Lights Out

A Historical Journal

The Sacred Journey of Restoring Hawaiian Values to Waikiki

Published by
Carlino & Company
Honolulu, Hawaii

Published by
Carlino & Company
P.O. Box 15182
Honolulu, Hawaii 96830
(808) 926-1752
carlinog@hotmail.com

ISBN: 0-937827-06-1

First Printing August 2013

Front cover: Hawaii State Archives, *Honolulu Star-Advertiser* collection, photo by Richard Walker taken on October 4, 1994

Design, typography and print production by
Blaine Fergerstrom, ZZ-Type, Honolulu, Hawaii

You may purchase additional copies of this book at:
www.LightsOutBook.com

Visit our other websites at:
www.TheArtOfLettingGo.com
www.BeliefsWithoutBorders.com
www.GolfMagic.us
www.TheLandOfAloha.com
www.Carlino.us

This book is dedicated to the Hawaiian people in hopes that it will contribute to the protection and preservation of their heritage.

Sincere thanks to Bacco Mulligano for editing the call-to-action messages; the late Carlos Arévalo-Gómez for suggesting the "Lights Out" rallying call; Kate Kincaid for editing this book; and Luella Kurkjian, Historical Records Branch Chief at the Hawaii State Archives, for assistance in obtaining the front cover photo.

BELIEF PRECEDES EXPERIENCE. These three words were the foundation for our call-to-action messages which began on June 22, 1988.

The light structures on Kalakaua Avenue were indicative of an oppressive governmental belief system toward the indigenous Hawaiian culture. The $13.2 million dollar renovation of Waikiki in 1988 was a project that turned good citizens into indifferent citizens and indifferent citizens into alienated citizens. It also turned socially concerned citizens into activists.

Some people may ask why the light structures are a Hawaiian issue. *There are no boundaries as to what shape or form symbols of oppression may take, and the light structures were representative of an* ***indifferent attitude*** *toward the indigenous Hawaiian culture.* The issue went beyond whether citizens liked or disliked the visual image of the light structures. The consciousness of what they represented translated into alienation—as well as the pain, suffering, and violence that goes with it—for the Hawaiian people.

The first step towards achieving liberation from such negative forces comes with the recognition of reality. In order to rectify a situation, we must first acknowledge that a problem exists. In the case of the light structures, we were presented with a symbol of the oppression that continued to plague the Hawaiian people. What follows is an account of reactions by Hawaiian and non-Hawaiian citizens, the media, and government officials and the reality that they represented.

After the first call-to-action messages in the newspapers on June 22, 1988, certain questions became vitally important. *The light structures had* ***overthrown*** *all hope of having a Hawaiian ambience on Kalakaua Avenue, a street that is the Hawaiians' main showcase for the preservation of their culture and heritage to visitors from around the world.* Was this ignoble action an instance of history repeating itself? Would the population respond differently than the population of a century before when an entire government was overthrown?

What would be the media's role? Would they be thorough in pursuing the reasons behind such a degrading action toward the Hawaiian people and their culture? Would the media somehow instill confidence in the Hawaiian people to reverse the government's disgraceful action?

Would the mayor have the courage to admit his grave mistake and be willing to endure the embarrassment of removing the structures? In the midst of a re-election campaign, would his fundamental question be, "What is the best course of action for the Hawaiian people?" or would it be, "What is the best course of action for my political campaign?"

What would be the role of the Hawaiian Democratic governor? The mayor, once Democrat but turned Republican, was considered by some to be the young governor's mentor. Would the governor's political loyalty and friendship with the mayor take precedence over concerns for the dignity of his own people and heritage?

What course of action would elected officials, state legislature, and city council take? The Hawaii Visitors Bureau?

The Outdoor Circle? The hotel owners? What about non-Hawaiians?

The most important response would have to come from the Hawaiian people. The question of the light structures went beyond basic survival issues for the Hawaiian people and their culture; it did not involve land, housing, or fishing rights. It primarily involved concepts such as beliefs and consciousness. Had Hawaiians abandoned Waikiki? Would they respond?

In an era of "open government," the installation of the light structures on Kalakaua Avenue had taken the entire community, including the media, by surprise. For many people the words "Hawai'i" and "beauty" are synonymous, but for many these structures were totally incongruent with the natural beauty of this land.

Our initial response to the installation was one of anger toward the marring of this magnificent land's physical beauty. The course of action for expressing our anger would be the written word, and daily newspapers would be the means to convey our message. It was then that the message **"KALAKAUA EYESORE"** was written and submitted for publication in the two daily newspapers. The message suggested that readers call the mayor and ask him to "replace these monstrosities with something to reflect the charm of the islands."

A constructive expression of anger can increase awareness and lift veils that mask the reality of a situation.

Following the submission of the message for publication, it became clear that the issue went far beyond the structures' lack of physical beauty. The words "Belief Precedes Experience" became more meaningful. The fundamental question for us became, "What would a government have to believe in, in order to create this reality?"

It was obvious that the oppressive government consciousness toward the Hawaiian people that had existed for nearly a century still existed when the light structures were installed. *The government had two choices with reference to this extremely important renovation project. They could look to the Hawaiian peo-*

ple and their culture for inspiration, or they could completely ignore the Hawaiians. The government chose the latter.

The light structures on Kalakaua Avenue had two clear characteristics. First, the government's beliefs and attitudes toward the Hawaiian people were an integral part of these highly visible structures. What the structures represented could not be covered up. Secondly, these structures removed the illusion that the government deeply cared for the Hawaiian people and their heritage. *The light structures were no longer metal, paint, glass or electrical wires, but rather a window for viewing the government's consciousness toward the Hawaiian people.* To say that the color of the light structures represented Hawaiian tapa was the government's desperate attempt to keep an illusion alive.

A study of state statistics revealed a surprising reality—nearly 200,000 people in the state claimed to have at least 1% Native Hawaiian blood. There were choices before us. Should we go behind the scenes to discuss our concerns to a few of these Hawaiians, or should we present our beliefs as an open issue to which Hawaiians could freely respond? The message **"HAWAIIANS UNITE"** was written, and it suggested that, "The Renaissance of Waikiki must be a Hawaiian Renaissance." It urged Hawaiians not to tolerate the desecration of Waikiki and said, "Let 100,000 march along Kalakaua Avenue. And march again until the tide of disgrace is reversed. Say 'LIGHTS OUT' now before it's too late." The message was given to the daily newspapers for simultaneous publication with the **"KALAKAUA EYESORE"** message, and both messages were printed on June 22, 1988.

The plan was simple. Have 100,000 Hawaiians march down Kalakaua Avenue in unity to demonstrate their desire to put an end to a government that had dominated, manipulated, and instilled fear in them for far too long. A fifteen-minute walk from Gateway Park to Kapiolani Park could have instantly sparked the government's decision to remove the culturally degrading light structures. Even if only 1% (2,000) of the Hawaiian population had responded, the results would have been the same.

That victory, with its great show of strength by the Hawaiian people, could have been the foundation for an effort to end other injustices affecting the Hawaiian community. Within weeks, 100 years of an oppressive consciousness toward the Hawaiian people could have started to dissolve.

Some government officials believed that Hawaii's visitors did not care about the Hawaiian people and their culture, and that only the basics of Hawaiian culture should be preserved as the state moved into the future. Those erroneous beliefs could have been challenged by a highly visible demonstration.

Unfortunately there was no response to the call for a march down Kalakaua Avenue. Would the Hawaiian people wait months to respond, much like their ancestors who waited for 15 months after their government was overthrown, only to be resoundingly defeated? An immediate response could have resulted in an immediate victory for the Hawaiian people. Were they not ultimately responsible for their own heritage?

The morning newspaper, *The Honolulu Advertiser,* called us for an interview. *We reluctantly agreed in hopes that the inter-*

view would spark action. The role of non-Hawaiians should be to support Hawaiians in their choice of action. The decision to end the dishonor and the leadership it required had to come from the Hawaiian population. Otherwise, there would be no true end to government's oppressive consciousness toward the Hawaiian people.

In an article that appeared in the morning newspaper on June 25, 1988, the mayor's Director of Transportation questioned our motives for placing the call-to-action messages. Throughout the election campaign of the next several months, the mayor praised him as a valuable member of the team. Yet one month after the mayor's victory, he was fired. Strangely, there was no media coverage relating his elimination to the multi-million dollar renovation of Waikiki or the installation of the light structures.

Many people in Hawaii avoid Waikiki, and they do so for a multitude of reasons. The first step in solving any problem is creating awareness that a problem exists. *We hoped the next two call-to-action messages would unite non-Hawaiians as a support group for the Hawaiian people. More importantly, we hoped they would elicit a response from Hawaiians regarding the outrage against their heritage.* The first message, printed on July 3, 1988, was entitled **"WHEN WAS THE LAST TIME YOU VISITED WAIKIKI?"** It asked readers to visit Waikiki and call the mayor and request that the light structures be removed. The second message was headlined **"PEOPLE OF HAWAII: BREAK THE SILENCE"** and was published three days later. It quoted the words of the poet Kahlil Gibran, "And as a single leaf turns not yellow but with the silent knowledge of the whole tree, so the wrong-doer cannot do wrong without the hidden will of you all." Again, it suggested readers call the mayor and stand up, speak up, and say "Lights Out."

The mayor's office began receiving numerous calls. The first official response was denial—they were not responsible for the light structures. It subsequently became evident that the fundamental question for the city administration was, "What is the best course of action for our political campaign?"

Letters to the editor began appearing in the daily newspapers, and continued through the next several months.

The media's beliefs began taking shape, and it was clear there would be very little support for the Hawaiian people. The afternoon newspaper, *The Honolulu Star-Bulletin*, stated in an editorial that they liked the "big" structures. Some 16 months later the newspaper devoted more space and showed greater concern for the controversy surrounding a mascot for the University of Hawaii football team than they gave to the issue of the light structures. Belief guides action. The morning newspaper was content in creating a debate in the "Letter to the Editor" section, and it wasn't until sixteen months later that an editorial appeared stating that the renovation of Waikiki was a "success." *Only Don Chapman, a lone columnist for the morning newspaper, had the courage to repeatedly write about the controversial light structures.*

A popular radio personality wrote in his weekly newspaper article that those who don't like the light structures should complain instead about where they lived before moving to paradise.

We declined interviews when television reporters called. Our reply was that we believed this issue affected Hawaiians and their culture, and that it would be more appropriate to interview representatives from the Hawaiian population. The response of one concerned reporter was startling. "Hawaiians will not do anything. This issue will die." Low expectations such as these had always plagued Hawaiians, especially Hawaiian children. How can children perform to their highest potential when their young minds are imprisoned by the prejudicial beliefs, attitudes, and low expectations of those in positions of power and authority?

Some radio talk shows called for interviews. We gave the same reply as was given to television stations.

Some non-Hawaiians called us claiming to be outraged at

the city's installation of the light structures, but their offers of support ended once the mayor announced that he was considering painting the structures.

Many people chose public silence. Every elected federal official remained silent. Every state legislator remained silent. Every city council member remained silent. The Hawaii Visitors Bureau, the Outdoor Circle, and hotel executives remained silent as well.

Even the Hawaiian governor remained silent.

One hotel executive called to suggest a particular course of action we could take. When we replied that he could undertake his own suggested plan, his response was, "Not me. I don't want to get involved." A year later a quote appeared in the newspaper: "No one dares to say what he really thinks. We all have to tell lies." The quote was from a young Chinese student after the Tiananmen Square massacre in China, yet it very well could have been from a citizen of a free country where fear and mistrust of government exists, and where the media does not uphold its responsibility to the people.

July 29, 1988 was the date set for the celebration of the Kalakaua Avenue renovation project. The day before the event, the city announced that they would remove panels from certain light structures to "lighten up" the look. On July 29 the mayor announced the city would look into the possibility of painting the structures. It was an excellent political move that placated many people.

The morning newspaper took the city's actions as a personal victory. The messages in the newspaper had generated calls to the mayor's office. City officials had noted letters to the editor. Public pressure had forced the city to respond. A reporter called for us to come to Waikiki and have our photo taken next to a light structure. We declined the invitation.

What value would any of the city's actions have on restoring respect and dignity to Hawaiians and their heritage? Painting the light structures would be a literal and figurative cover up. It would do nothing to change the beliefs that allowed the installation of the light structures. The root cause of the problem would not be cured. By the end of 1988 the light structures remained unpainted. The media had no further word on the subject.

Nearly 100,000 people attended the block party for the celebration of the Kalakaua Avenue renovation project. The city used Hawaiian entertainers to promote the party. What if these Hawaiian entertainers had refused to perform until the city replaced the light structures? This would have been a tremendous act of courage, and the entertainers could have become heroes to the Hawaiian people.

This was a time to examine our own belief system—a time to conquer our own fears. *It was a time to strengthen our resolve and renew our commitment to help protect and preserve Hawaii's indigenous culture.*

On August 3, 1988 three messages titled **CULTURAL DISGRACE, HAWAIIANS UNITE**, and **KAMEHAMEHA: WHERE ARE YOU?** were placed together and submitted to the daily newspapers. The first message included the mayor's response to citizens' concerns over this issue in which he stated, "The cost of the poles, fixtures and installation amounted to $650,000. The installation of the electrical system, which includes the fire alarm system and removal of the old system, cost an additional $1.45 million. Thus the cost to replace these traffic modules and street lights would be prohibitive." The message concluded with our reply. "Should not the response of the people be just as clear? THE DIGNITY OF HAWAIIAN CULTURE BEARS NO PRICE TAG!" The second message, **HAWAIIANS UNITE**, was the same as the original message of June 22. The third message began by asking, "Who will stand up to lead the Hawaiian people against this blatant act of cultural aggression?"

The city administration formulated a position paper to respond to the numerous calls to city hall. After all that had been taken away from Hawaiians over the years, how could Hawaiian heritage be ignored with the excuse that the price tag was too high? An article in the newspapers spoke of a Japanese friend of the mayor who offered the city $4,900,000 for improvements if he was granted certain development rights. Were there not other friends who would contribute to this cause?

The city administration's position paper mentioned that numerous organizations were consulted about the light structures, but not a single organization was Hawaiian. Were there designers, architects, or planners who had a vision of creating a Hawaiian ambience for this project? Were they isolated and cut off from this project? It is one thing to attempt a Hawaiian ambience and not achieve the desired outcome. *It is another to completely ignore the indigenous culture.*

Some people who have dealt with government on various projects realize that meetings, even public ones, are frequently a façade. The major decisions have often already been made behind the scenes. Were some of the organizations listed as having been consulted manipulated by the city into sharing responsibility for the light structures? Was the silence of these organizations a way to avoid further involvement in a project that took even them by surprise?

The Hawaiian people could not have hoped to end their oppression unless they united and spoke with one voice. The newspapers were reporting on dissension within the ranks of trustees at the Office of Hawaiian Affairs, the largest organized Hawaiian body. At a much later date (September 14, 1989, *The Honolulu Advertiser*, Page A-5), one Hawaiian individual publicly referred to the majority of these trustees as "bastards" who had broken their responsibility to Hawaiians of 50% or more Hawaiian blood.

What was the origin of mistrust between the Hawaiian people and their leaders? Could it date back nearly 200 years to the unification of the Hawaiian Islands when brother fought brother? Though the unification ended the fighting between chiefs of the various islands, could the pain of that unification still be unresolved? Could people back then have predicted the future—that their government would eventually be overthrown and the Hawaiian culture would be all but erased?

How could a government be overthrown, even by force, unless the people felt underlying isolation and abandonment by their standing government? How could Hawaiians lose total control of Waikiki, a place that was one of their most important cultural centers on Oahu, unless they had abandoned or isolated themselves from it? Some Hawaiians resented the influx of visitors because of how that growth had negatively impacted their land. But feelings of anger, hurt, and pain do not absolve anyone from responsibility.

The mayoral campaign was entering its final month. Many people realize that in the last few weeks and days before an election, politicians do things they would not do at other times throughout the campaign. Though the issue of preserving the Hawaiian culture should transcend all political consideration, the political setting was available. Would the Hawaiian people take advantage of the opportunity?

At the end of September we overheard a tour bus operator refer to the light structures as "industrial lights," and he seemed to say this with a sense of pride. His words became the basis for the next message. *Some saw the light structures as displays of pride; we believed them to be symbols of oppression.* The government's actions were already having a cancerous effect on Hawaiian culture as experienced by visitors who came to Hawaii. What would these actions do to the next generation of Hawaiians?

On October 5, 1988 we placed our next message, **INDUSTRIAL LIGHTS SYMBOLS OF OPPRESSION**, in the daily papers. The message said, "As always, it is the children who suffer most from oppression. Must another generation of Hawaiians grow up with MINDS shackled, held in bondage by the actions of an uncaring government? Will the next generation look back at these lights with a sense of sorrow and defeat, and simply add them to the long list of injustices already inflicted upon Hawaiians? Or will they recall with PRIDE that the REMOVAL of these Industrial Lights was a significant step in their continuing sacred journey of preserving at all costs, their unique and precious identity?"

The mayor's political campaign was victorious. While the campaign boasted about the renovation of Waikiki, not one of the television or print ads showed images of the light structures.

The mayor owed a debt of gratitude to the governor. The governor's silence had virtually assured the mayor his victory, though at the expense of the dignity and respect of the Hawaiian people. Yet in a sense it proved to be a hollow victory. The mayor, who had voiced aspirations to be governor, never challenged the governor in a gubernatorial election.

It seemed that Hawaiians suffered the most under the leadership of their own people. In the 19th century, the greatest dissolution of Hawaiian culture and the takeover of Hawaiian land by foreigners occurred under the reign of Hawaiian rulers. In the 20th century history was repeating itself.

The silence of politicians and media organizations continued. Often silence is the loudest sound heard. *Was silence a way to keep waters calm?*

Some say time is a great healer. In fact it is not time, but actions of individuals that create healing. Waiting for time to heal often only delays the healing process. The Memorial Day weekend was an appropriate opportunity for the next message.

May of 1989 approximately marked the first anniversary of the massive mainland light structures in Waikiki. On May 26 a message was published in the daily newspapers with the headline **A MEMORIAL REMEMBRANCE**. Part of the message said, "The degrading and humiliating light structures on Kalakaua Avenue will be uprooted and removed – and with them a negative consciousness toward the Hawaiian people that never again will gain a foothold in this land. And a NEW LIGHT will dawn upon Waikiki – a LIGHT that will glow in harmony with the majestic Moana Hotel. And the new and appropriately elegant Hawaiian lamp poles will be a clear signal to millions of visitors and to people throughout the world that here in Waikiki, we are truly in the midst of a rebirth of Hawaiian culture, pride and dignity."

The restoration of the Moana Hotel, Waikiki's oldest hotel, was completed. The light structures on Kalakaua Avenue were totally incongruent with what the restoration represented, and the contrast was clear. Beliefs and attitudes form the foundation for decisions. What if the beliefs and attitudes of government officials had been in harmony with the intentions of the hotel's restoration team? Would not a different reality for Hawaiians have been created? The majestic Moana Hotel appeared imprisoned by the garish light structures that surrounded it.

Though the restoration of the Moana Hotel and the installation of the Kalakaua Avenue light structures were diametrically opposed projects, they did share one common element—beliefs. Just as beliefs form the foundation for the shape of an individual's life, beliefs were the framework for 200,000 people.

The beliefs that guided the Moana Hotel restoration continued to lead to healing, growth, and the eventual preservation of Hawaiian heritage. The beliefs that guided the installation of the light structures continued to lead to pain, oppression, and the eventual destruction of a great part of Hawaiian heritage.

The state legislature, which could have played a very important role in helping the Hawaiian people, instead appropriated $70,000 for a conference to discuss future plans for Waikiki. Were not the unresolved pain and oppression of the past integral parts of the future? Do pain and oppression end by pretending they do not exist? The most grandiose plans for Waikiki would only have had a minimal effect on the Hawaiian people's present dilemma.

Creating new beginnings from a sense of freedom results in a movement toward joy. Creating new beginnings to avoid pain or oppression only results in a continuation of those problems.

In order for pain and oppression to be reversed, responsible citizens had to demand that their government live up to its responsibilities toward its citizens. They also had to demand that the media recognize and act upon its obligation to support preservation of the Hawaiian culture.

Mainland television executives privately ridiculed the light structures and their adverse impact on Waikiki, yet on their television broadcasts references to Waikiki were just the opposite. It was hypocrisy and they knew it. The hypocrisy continued as long as the government refused to take action.

Watching a friend suffer pain can be as difficult as experiencing your own pain. *The next message was the most difficult one to write.*

On July 23, 1989, the 1,500-plus word message **AN OPEN LETTER TO THE HAWAIIANS** was submitted and printed in the two daily newspapers. Here is the paid message in its entirety.

"The value you place in your ancestry, in its delicate yet powerful MANA will determine the path you will follow into the future. Your dignity and your destiny are one and the same thing. Last year, when the massive culturally degrading light structures were installed along Kalakaua Avenue you received yet another severe blow to your sense of self-worth, an echo to the **seeds of pain** planted long ago in your people when your culture was nearly destroyed.

Now you feel betrayed once again, betrayed by government, business and media leaders whom you have entrusted to help protect the identity and integrity of your heritage – and those **seeds of pain** are buried deep within these light structures. The sudden change in your reality has created a sense of aloneness and detachment from the aesthetics of your heritage – and those **seeds of pain** are buried deep within these light structures. Your sense of justice has been breached by a $13.2 million dollar renovation project intended to enhance the image of this state to millions of visitors from around the world, a project conceived and executed as if 200,000 Hawaiians did not exist – and those **seeds of pain** are buried deep within these light structures.

That **pain** spans across several generations. From your kupuna who have almost become numbed to responding due to the witnessing of so many injustices, to your keiki whose young minds have become shackled by the actions of government.

You know within your heart that these structures must be removed. For if there is one important lesson you have learned either individually or in the course of your history, it is that the seeds of pain – **not removed** – will sprout and grow and be the seeds of **future pain**. (And that pain is accelerating. For when the convention center controversy has been resolved, you and your children will be called upon to lure millions of visitors to keep the center filled, and yet you have no assurance the center will be uniquely Hawaiian.)

Also buried deep within these light structures is the **oppressive consciousness** of government toward your heritage. **Belief precedes action.** A simple truth. These government officials are entrapped by this consciousness that has been in existence far too long. Just recently, after more than a year, three light structures on Kalakaua Avenue were uprooted and removed. This action is **significant** for it is representative of a government that reacts to pressure rather than taking the lead in doing what is just. A government that hopes its citizens may become too weary to take continued action. And most importantly, a government that **privately** understands it has made a grave mistake against your heritage yet continues to **publicly** defend these structures at the expense of your dignity and respect. Their weaknesses must not become your weaknesses. Of greater importance is your own system of beliefs and attitudes, thoughts and feelings, choices and decisions. For when you change **your own consciousness** you simultaneously change the consciousness of government.

There are many among you who feel the **spiritual** separation these structures represent for your heritage and you have a **vision** of new Hawaiian lamp poles which would place you in communion and harmony with your MANA. **Yet why have you remained silent?** What are you avoiding? What is the fear? What is the guarantee you are holding out for but cannot have? Why has your self-pity become so important to you? Cast aside any obstacles in your way, for you have the tools necessary to remove these structures. They are Desire, Imagination and Expectation. **You need no others.**

You may ask why we as non-Hawaiians have placed **seven** messages in this paper concerning this issue. It is not our intention to cause discord. In fact, just the opposite – a simple desire to help **end** the pain and the struggle. The true reason for our attitude lies perhaps in a deeper meaning in your word **"Ohana"**. For though we are strangers and guests in your land, you have extended to us the invaluable gift of **friendship** and let us share in the bounty of your islands. Your MANA still rules this land and **no government** can take that Power away from you. And we all share in the joys that bring you closer to that **liberating** realization as well as the **sorrows** that may take you further away.

Non-Hawaiians cannot ultimately make the decision to remove these structures from your land. For this issue is far beyond that of the lack of physical beauty. **This issue involves your own sacred journey and your relationship with your MANA.** As such the decision must be yours. And the decision to **replace** these structures must also be yours.

Like the government, you have choices. You can continue to take no action. You can **mask** the pain by pretending you have not been betrayed or by thinking: "Why make waves?

Why rock the boat? And there are other ways to mask the pain. You can **deny** that these structures have separated you from the aesthetics of your heritage. Or you can **ignore** these structures and hope the trees may cover them during the day and darkness cover them at night, and maybe no one will notice the pain. Or you can **numb** yourself to the pain by abandoning Waikiki as if it were not a part of your land and a dwelling place of your MANA. And yet you know that pain masked, denied, ignored or numbed continues to grow.

Or you have this choice, the one and only real choice: to begin to end the pain, to **declare** and **demand** your right as Hawaiians to have these structures **removed** from your land. You can end the embarrassment of partying and parading under structures that have deadened the senses of millions of visitors toward your heritage and that have attempted to murder the passion of your dignity and respect. You can show your strength and end the role of **victimhood.** You can take back your Power by refusing to blame others and understanding you are **responsible** for your reality by **allowing** this to happen. You can embark upon a journey that will replace these structures with ones that will be in harmony with your MANA. You will succeed. **For if three structures can be removed – they can all be removed.** You know that any placating or cover-up action by government officials will not end the pain. They may increase the visibility of your singers and dancers or improve the attractiveness of the surrounding land - and the seeds of pain **will still remain.** They may cover these structures with thousands of gallons of paint with a new color that will glitter in the sun and dazzle your eyes – and the seeds of pain **will still remain.**

There are those among you who have **courageously** accepted the challenge of protecting your heritage at all costs. And your successful actions have been an **inspiration** and, of course, a benefit to **all** Hawaiians, and to those who have a profound respect for your heritage. Yet not withstanding your successes, the pain continues. The struggle continues.

Will you ever **unite?** Will you ever **unite?** Is it time **now** to unite? Is it time now to **forgive** yourself and those who have betrayed you? Is it time now to say "LIGHTS OUT"? There are no leaders to guide you. Each of you must be your own leader. Nearly 200,000 of you claim Hawaiian blood. In self-examination what does that mean in a **spiritual** sense? And does not the honor of being Hawaiian carry with it a **responsibility?** And for those who are multi-ethnic and not predominately Hawaiian is it not clear that an injustice against one race is an injustice against all races for you cannot divide yourself **spiritually**.

Should your asking to have these structures removed be refused and you continue to be dominated, would it not then be appropriate to take visible action? What if 1,000, 10,000, or 100,000 Hawaiians marched down Kalakaua Avenue to demonstrate your desire to end **not only** the **oppressive consciousness** that these structures symbolize, but also to end the **many other injustices** which touch upon your community? And what if your own **political leaders** participated in the march? Would that change the levels of consciousness of all levels of government toward your heritage? Would it change the consciousness of millions of people around the world toward your heritage? Would it change **your own consciousness** toward your heritage?

The massive culturally degrading light structures on Kalakaua Avenue **don't lie!!!** For as long as you allow, they will continue to be a visible reminder of a government's **oppressive consciousness**, and of your own **separation from** and **longing for** spiritual harmony. And their removal **will** signify a turnaround and a spiritual renewal sparked by your tenacious desire to maintain a strong bond with your MANA.

Once you truly begin that **sacred journey** how could a small group of government officials ever again dominate or culturally disgrace 200,000 Hawaiians? How could a government ever again culturally shackle the minds of your young children? And who can criticize you if you break off those chains in your quest for kūʻokoʻa? Is it time **now** to begin that sacred journey to **end** the pain and the struggle? Is it time **now** to say "LIGHTS OUT"? The final decision is yours."

No response from the Hawaiian people. Did they not care? Or did they feel tired and helpless, trapped in their pain from so many years of abuse and oppression? *Was the issue of "light structures" one injustice too many in which to become involved?*

Hawaiians protested to prevent hotels being built over their burial places, to stop freeways being built over their religious temples, to stop industrial plants being built on their sacred lands, to stop the Navy's bombing on the island of Kahoolawe. Why did the suffering of Hawaiians have to continue?

On August 29, 1989 we wrote a letter to the mayor and delivered it to his office. A few years prior, the mayor had shared with citizens the story of his own spiritual rebirth, a journey that he said added fulfillment and wholeness to his life. In the letter, we asked the following questions among others: "Why deny the Hawaiians that same sacred journey? Will the massive culturally degrading light structures on Kalakaua Avenue be a part of your legacy to the Hawaiian people? Are you ready to help end the pain and the struggle of the Hawaiian people? Are you ready to say 'LIGHTS OUT'?"

The mayor chose not to respond.

The following year the celebration for completing the Waikiki renovation project was being promoted as the "Waikiki Summer Block Party." *History gets distorted when governments and business leaders attempt to cover up their own shame, and when the media lacks the integrity to report the truth.*

The next message in the daily newspapers was an attempt to remind everyone of the real purpose for the celebration, and more importantly, to discourage Hawaiians from participating in the celebration of a project that had shamed their heritage.

The message was placed in the daily newspapers on June 12, 1990, and was entitled **CELEBRATE???** The message began by asking the question, "Is there really reason to celebrate this week when people will gather to commemorate the $13.2 million dollar renovation of Waikiki?" And ended by saying, "Is it time for Hawaiians from each of the islands to come together united by all of their struggles, and to walk down Kalakaua Avenue as a means of declaring to the world that this Old Consciousness does not have a place in this Sacred Land? Walk in love – a way to let go and break the negative patterns of the Past."

The Hawaiian people took no action.

Although it is non-Hawaiians who have fundamentally caused the decline of Hawaiian heritage, it is Hawaiians who have allowed their heritage to decline. On September 24, 1990, we wrote a letter to Native Hawaiian governor John Waihee. The Governor chose silence, and on October 29, 1990, we decided to reprint the letter in the daily newspapers. The letter was simply titled **DEAR JOHN.**

The letter contained twenty-three questions including, "Was the $13.2 million dollar renovation of Waikiki an act of love toward Hawaiians and their heritage?"; "Does the project show respect for Hawaiian culture?"; and "Does it show a sense of caring and commitment for the protection and preservation of Hawaiian heritage?" It ended by saying, "When the Governor chooses to respond, his complete response will be printed in this paper. We deserve to know the depth of the Governor's consciousness."

The Governor chose to remain silent.

We continued placing messages in the newspapers on a yearly basis until 1999, seventeen in all from when we first began. *The yearly messages were reminders of one more great assault on Hawaiian heritage, and of the fact that a heritage can die when an apathetic majority allows an aggressive, uncaring minority to have its way.* They were also a reminder of the importance of creating an ambience on Kalakaua Avenue worthy of the dignity and respect of Hawaiian heritage.

On May 10, 1999, a new law was created that outlined objectives for the Waikiki Special District. It contained language that would "promote a Hawaiian sense of place at every opportunity" and "promote a sense of 'Hawaiianness' within the district." It further stated that, "The design of buildings and structures in the Waikiki Special District should always reflect a Hawaiian sense of place."

The Hawaiian people were the driving force in creating that law.

In the summer of 2000, the culturally oppressive light structures on Kalakaua Avenue were completely removed. This was a momentous action towards the rebirth of Hawaiian culture, pride and dignity, and the restoration of Hawaiian values in Waikiki. It signified a dramatic change in the belief system regarding Hawaiian heritage. We reflected on the words written in our May 26, 1989, message. "The degrading and humiliating light structures on Kalakaua Avenue will be uprooted and removed – and with them a negative consciousness toward the Hawaiian people that never again will gain a foothold in this land."

www.ingramcontent.com/pod-product-compliance
Lightning Source LLC
LaVergne TN
LVHW050950080826
845145LV00004B/1460

* 9 7 8 0 9 3 7 8 2 7 0 6 2 *